On the edge

# Back Off!

Folens

United Kingdom: Folens Publishers, Apex Business Centre, Boscombe Road, Dunstable, LU5 4RL.
Email: folens@folens.com

Ireland: Folens Publishers, Greenhills Road, Tallaght, Dublin 24.
Email: info@folens.ie

Poland: JUKA, ul. Renesansowa 38, Warsaw 01-905.



Editor: Joanne Mitchell

Layout artist: Suzanne Ward

Cover design: John Hawkins

First published 2005 by Folens Limited.



British Library Cataloguing in Publication Data. A catalogue record for this publication is available from the British Library.

ISBN 1 84303 729 7

# Contents

# The story so far

**If you haven't read an *On the edge* book before:**
The stories take place in and around a row of shops and buildings called Pier Parade in Brightsea, right next to the sea. There's Big Fry, the fish and chip shop; Drop Zone, the drop-in centre for local teenagers; Macmillan's, the sweet and souvenir shop; Anglers' Haven, the fishing tackle shop; the Surf 'n' Skate shop and, of course, the Brightsea Beach Bar.

**If you have read an *On the edge* book** you may have met some of these people before.

| | |
|---|---|
| *Becky Macmillan:* | *her mum runs Macmillan's, the sweet and souvenir shop.* |
| *Jan:* | *her older sister.* |
| *Em Mistry:* | *Jan's friend.* |
| *Lee Wood:* | *a boy from Becky's school.* |
| *Tom Burton:* | *the owner of Surf 'n' Skate.* |

**So, what's been going on?**
Becky tries to be a good kid, but things don't always work out. Her best friend Trudy has left the school and Becky feels lonely. Her older sister is at 'big school' and dad isn't around much, so life isn't easy.

**What happens in this story?**
Becky's new 'friend' Lee pressurises her about stealing from the Surf 'n' Skate shop, and Becky is tempted. After all, at least Lee is her friend, isn't he?

# Characters

BECKY MACMILLAN

JAN MACMILLAN: Becky's sister

EM MISTRY: Jan's friend

LEE WOOD: Becky's friend

TOM BURTON: owner of Surf 'n' Skate

# Scene 1

**The Surf 'n' Skate shop.**

*Late afternoon.*

*BECKY and LEE are standing near the door.*

BECKY: I like this T-shirt.

LEE: It's the same as your sister's.

BECKY: She looks good in it too.

LEE: Go on, Becky, nick it.

BECKY: What?!

LEE: You're scared, aren't you?

*BECKY picks up a T-shirt.*

LEE: Go on, quick! There's no one around.

BECKY: I really like it.

LEE: Put it in your bag. Quick! Go on, quick!

*BECKY starts to put the T-shirt in her bag. She stops. She puts it back.*

LEE (*quietly*):
Too late now, stupid.

TOM: What can I do for you two, then?

LEE: Nice T-shirts.

TOM: They're half price. A good deal. If you've got the money that is.

LEE: We've got money. Plenty. But … we'll think about it.

BECKY: Lee, I've got to go. I'll be late.

LEE: Maybe we'll come back tomorrow. See ya, Tom.

*TOM watches as they leave.*

# Scene 2

*Next day.*

*BECKY and LEE are sitting on the beach near the Surf 'n' Skate shop.*

LEE: You're so stupid, Becky. That T-shirt could be yours now.

BECKY: So? What did *you* take?

LEE (*laughing*):
You think I can't?

BECKY: You, you're all talk.

LEE: Look what I've got then.

BECKY: A torch! Where did you get that?

LEE: I got it in town.

BECKY: Where?

LEE: Not telling.

BECKY: Bet you didn't take it.

LEE: Don't care what you think.

*LEE dances around her.*

BECKY: Stop shining that thing in my eyes.

LEE: Dare you! Dare you!

BECKY: Get off, Lee!

LEE: Chicken! Chicken!

BECKY: You just wait here, then.

*BECKY goes into the Surf 'n' Skate shop. She soon comes back.*

BECKY: See!

LEE: So you've got the T-shirt. Easy innit?

BECKY: C'mon. Let's clear off.

LEE: Thief! Thief! Think Tom'll catch you?

# Scene 3

**The Macmillans' shop.**

*Three days later.*

*JAN is closing up her mum's shop. Her friend EM is with her.*

JAN: She's a pain in the neck.

EM: Who? Becky?

JAN: Yes, my little sister Becky!

EM: But she looks up to you.

JAN: You mean she wants my clothes! I found her yesterday wearing my T-shirt.

EM: What did you do?

JAN: What d'you think?

EM: You're so hard on her, Jan.

JAN: What? Me? She ran off wearing my T-shirt! She's been funny lately anyway. Acting odd.

EM: How d'you mean?

JAN: She's been hanging around with Lee Wood.

EM: Lee Wood. Who's he?

JAN: He's older than Becky. He's always in trouble.

EM: Trouble? That's not like Becky. (*joking*) It's more like you.

*JAN looks at her, hands on hips.*

JAN: Thanks for those few kind words, Em. I'll ignore them.

EM: All the same, it's odd about Becky.

JAN: Well, if she gets up to anything, I'll be for it. I'm supposed to play big sister.

# Scene 4

**The Macmillans' shop.**

*Next day.*

*JAN is in the back room. EM has just come in.*

JAN: Look at this lot!

EM: Where did you get all that?

JAN: It's not mine. It's Becky's.

EM: Hair slides, sweets, nail varnish, pens, DVDs. It goes on and on.

JAN: And note the T-shirt. Just like mine.

EM: So she wasn't wearing yours the other day?

JAN: Doesn't look like it. I thought it fitted rather too well.

EM: Where did you find all this?

JAN: In her bag. She sometimes leaves it here.

EM: You went into her bag?

JAN: No, it was on that chair. It fell off. Everything tipped out. But it's worse than this, Em.

EM: Why?

JAN: My purse is missing. There were three notes in it … new notes.

EM: You think it's Becky?

JAN: I left it in the kitchen this morning. When I went back it wasn't there.

EM: Did you look for it?

JAN: Of course, Em. It's gone.

EM: And you think it was her?

JAN: It has to be her.

*Suddenly they hear a noise outside at the back of the shop. They hide behind the door. It opens.*

# Scene 5

**The Macmillans' shop.**

*Fifteen minutes later.*

*JAN, EM and BECKY are in the back room.*

JAN: Becky, that's no kind of answer. Let me ask you again. Where did you get this stuff?

BECKY: Back off – it's none of your business!

JAN: It will be if I tell mum. (*loudly*) And where's my money?

BECKY: What money?

JAN: The money in my purse.

BECKY: I haven't got it.

JAN: Don't lie.

EM: Right you two. Stop it. (*softly*) Becky tell us the truth.

BECKY: I can't.

EM: What's happened, Becky?

BECKY (*lip quivers*):
I can't say.

JAN (*loudly*):
What's going on, Rebecca?

BECKY: Back off, Jan!

EM (*softly*):
You can tell me.

BECKY: It's not my fault.

EM: Whose is it then?

BECKY: Well, it *is* me. But it's not *just* me.

JAN: It's that Lee Wood, isn't it?

*BECKY says nothing.*

JAN: Isn't it? I knew it. The little rat.

BECKY: He hasn't any friends. Neither have I.

EM (*quietly*): What do you mean, Becky?

BECKY: Since Trudy left I've got no real friends.

EM: But why go around with Lee Wood?

BECKY: I don't know. He does what he likes. No one cares about him.

JAN: What's she talking about?

EM: The thing is, Becky, you should take the stuff back.

BECKY: I can't!

EM: Well, take the T-shirt back. You like Tom don't you?

BECKY: Yeah.

EM: He'll be OK if you tell him the truth.

JAN (*loudly*): But what about my money?!

BECKY: That's nothing to do with me. Promise!

JAN: Why should I believe you?

BECKY: I've told you everything else.

EM: Leave it now, Jan.

JAN: It's easy for you to say. It's not your money. (*looking at BECKY)* If I find out it's you …

# Scene 6

**The Surf 'n' Skate shop.**

*Later, the same day.*

*LEE is looking at some T-shirts. But this time he's alone. TOM is watching him. He walks over to Lee.*

LEE: Nice T-shirts.

TOM: As I said the other day, they're half price.

LEE: I like this one.

TOM: A good deal – if you've got the money that is.

LEE: Who says I haven't?

TOM: Not me.

LEE: I've got money.

TOM: I'm sure you have.

LEE: I've got plenty. But … I'll think about it.

*LEE wanders towards the door, running his hand along the rail of T-shirts. He looks round to see if TOM is watching. He is. Then, changing his mind, LEE returns. He picks up the first T-shirt.*

LEE: I'll take this one.

*He hands TOM three new notes.*

# Glossary

| | |
|---|---|
| **(to) act odd/oddly** | (to) behave in a strange or unusual way |
| **(you're) all talk** | (you) say what you will do, but (you) don't do it |
| **back off!** | stop asking questions |
| **chicken** | coward |
| **(to) clear off** | (to) leave suddenly |
| **dare you!** | (I) challenge you (to do something) |
| **a good deal** | good value |
| **innit** | isn't it (impersonal/shortened form) |
| **(to) look up to someone** | (to) look to someone for guidance on how to behave |
| **nail varnish** | glossy paint for fingernails |
| **(to) nick** | (to) steal |
| **a pain in the neck** | someone who is irritating |
| **(to) play big sister** | (to) look after a younger child for your parents |
| **ya** | you (impersonal) |